FORBIDDEN

AURORA HART

FORBIDDEN

First published in Great Britain in 2024 by Sodaclown (Publishers)

ISBN 978-1-80517-990-0

To Gods, Devils, and Lovers x

CONTENTS

I

souls are fickle things, aren't they?

BREAKING YOU IN

you lay before me
stiff and unyielding
your myriad of treasure
hidden
underneath your fancy clothes

gazing upon your beauty
I run my hand over your skin
breath catching in my throat
while my fingertips slide underneath

I catch the merest glimpse of you
while my palm caresses along your sides
slowly I turn you around
and carefully run my fingers down your spine

in small, delicate flutters
I move back and forth along you
softening your edges
until eventually
you splay open
waiting for me to devour you

INTIMACY

---

your slender hips
nestled between my thighs
arm around your shoulders
knees and elbows pulling you so close
that every juddering breath of yours
echoes through my own rattling ribs

fingertips gently part
your most sacred of vessels
while you utter blasphemous prayers
to the night sky

I feel you
break
against me
in all your glory

and I sing your praises
to the dark
bringing you against my chest
as you quake and shudder

MOMENT

---

warm and soft from sleep
still covered in last night's kisses
I find the place where you rest your head
and bury myself in the scent of you
while gentle fluff
rumbles against my chest
and I hold grace in the palm of my hand

i listen to quiet acoustic strings
floating in the autumnal sun
wrapping myself in this moment, i am
content
and at home

AGONISING BLISS

lime green sliding in
slickened swollen pink
with a moan that shakes the gods
lost to the world
overcome by agonising waves of pleasure
as foundations crumble
and desperation screams through flesh
releasing a torrent of blissful torment

II

____

sometimes they're hellbent on destruction

KINTSUGI

---

can someone
hold these broken parts
while I
seal them with gold
you see
I wasn't careful with myself
and I
have learned that your affections
and your hatred
live in the same place
I can put me back together
but not without help
so I am begging
please
someone
hold me

RAZOR WIRE

---

constructing scaffolding around my heart
this precious thing
that beats inside my chest
that chokes me with blood
that takes my words
and wraps them over
and around my tongue
so they lay on the edge
straining to get out

this living creature fluttering in its cage
this soft
delicate
thing
no matter how many times it breaks
it never cements
instead, an aching
forever tender forever

too many people have thought this delicate thing
a plaything
a nothing
something

they aren't allowed near it

DROP

---

atomic universes slide off my fingertips
while molecules of you tear and bruise
seeping along scars
and burrowing through bones

delicately breaking apart
glass lined joints along leaded spines

cascades of light tearing through sinew
heaps of viscera at my feet

elbow deep in myself again
and it is so lonely here

REVENGE

---

whispers and smiles ensnare
passion pouring through determined lips
dilations declaring dominion
over parted thighs
slickly succumbing to sadistic fingertips
broken with desire
clinging to a life preserver
in the overwhelming
unending
waves

Nemesis smiles in remorseless revenge
capturing each limb in turn
drowning me in hubris
until
I
break

MOON EYES

---

lost in licentious labyrinths
flooded lights of cracked earth
rise through ash and ember
blinding blasphemous believers

bringing glittering obsidian spheres
crashing through space and time
entreating eternity to slip through shadow

while strangled tongues lift to the sky
stifling the softest of screams
in this chaotic cacophonous choir
of sunken seraphs

... BUT I WILL ANYWAY

I have no right to need you like this
unjust and crass
holding a beating bomb in both hands
with arterial spray dripping through my fingers

I have no right to want your attention
naked and bleating
making a hut of broken bones
held together with ink and shadow

I have no right to cry out in to the night
wailing and thrashing
lost to the echoes of myself
dissolved through the ache of time

HOLD ME

I crave
tight arms
wrapped around ribs
pulling me so close that I can barely breathe

I want to crawl under your skin
and wear you like a comfort blanket

.

I find the idea of gentleness
unsettling

There haven't been many
who desire to treat me tenderly

I'm terrified

to let someone hold my heart
and trust that they won't leave it battered

but I want to
I want to

DISSOLVE

---

find me
buried under my own excesses
find me
broken with love for you
find me
burrowed in the hole in my chest
find me
bent in my own agony
find me
before I fall apart

CITADELS

---

the duality of flesh and bone
against head and heart
separated
by miles of mortar and stone
resonating at breakneck frequencies

bodies crumble
so easily
anticipating
aches and agonies
delivered
so
exquisitely

while ancient ramparts
quietly shiver
and fracture
ever
so
slightly

shuddering through the soul of me

and every crack in this keep
feels like
the very world
breaking
under
my
feet

LONGING

---

a never ending babbling of nonsense
constantly flutters in my mind

I long for peace and quiet
but never can seem to find it
so quickly is it swallowed among
chaotic choruses
echoing
out of every last burrow

can we be quiet and still together please?

just lay in shadows, skin to skin?

only hearing breaths and whispers
the only sensation us against one another
fingertips along hips
skimming over skin
with lips pressed in to faces
and necks
and those fingertips
and.

I just need
to be
quietly
held

please.

COMING DOWN

---

bruises unfurl
deep within my core
softening me from within

I long to crawl under skin
to be held so close
that I don't exist any more

please
can I pour through you
please
hold me
while I break just a little
please
be a place
I can call home

III

____

some intrigue and terrify me in equal measure

SOFTLY

____

maybe you have just held
so many tender things
that you now handle them
instinctively

or maybe you're
(I think you might be)
the same
as me

SOULED

opening exoskeletons
to expose the soft
fleshy
shivering
innards

nerves screaming
buried in scarred tissue

settling in to the quiet gratitude
of the embrace of gentle hands
softly moving through the morass of broken flesh
occasionally pausing
before once again undertaking delicate deconstruction

tenderly seeking a concealed core
uncovering
layer
under
layer
discovering this fluttering
fragile
shadow
sealed in disarray

causing soft echoes of uncertainty
to slowly cease their protestations
as our souls find each other

INFERNAL COMMUNION

---

shadows dance around spines and
electricity sparks along limbs
as I cry out to our gods

suffused with insatiable torment
a palpable desire
I open myself unto them
freely offering a conduit

they descend and
smouldering waves wash over me
darkness slides in to me
cooling waters of the night dance along me
blackened flame pours through me
soothing the anguished longing
and bringing me back to myself
with an ungodly laugh
from this infernal communion

WITCH WEBS

searing, beautiful pain tearing through
skin tripped over by teeth
while digits dig and
disassemble desire in to a thousand tiny
pieces

the edge of you finds the edge of me and
"fuck" slips through lips in breathless response
with darkness thudding through hips
creating instinctive movements of moments
but slow, slow

slowly fingertips and lips find faces
eyes turned abyss
"there she is"
followed by grins sliding down lips
and flat palms on sternums

solid arms pulling close
softly kissing lips and tongues that were
ravaging not moments before
now keep everything held together
on the edge of disintegration

then these tongues and lips and fingertips
tease sensation from skin
eliciting pleasurable desperation
to watch eyes go black
as you are thrown over the edge
and lost to the void

victory is the taste of you
sliding hot
and sticky
in to the back of my throat

and settling for "fuck you"
and a surge of adrenaline
launching itself at me
bracing for a fight that never came

instead
being held so close
that I want to bury myself under your skin

brief respites
allow coalescence
before rising from the sweat soaked ashes
to find each other again
and again

until eventually you surrender

and it is here where we grow still

and whisper to one another
in the softest of breaths,
in a silent room
filled with soft light and Lust

ELECTRIC ENGINES

I want to run my fingertips
over the gyri under your cranium
skim along your parietal
and slowly tease the edges of you
from within

I would whisper to the temporal side of you
all of the things about you
that I adore
and then softly speak
of my most perverted longings

I want to bury my hands
deep inside your frontal lobe
learn what drives your tongue
find the synapse of
your happiest moment
trace the dendrites
that inspire words to tumble from your hands
and spill across digital pages
as I slide along axons
and find where their directions of impulse lead

NIGHT

ethereal shrouds surrounding
pulling twisting
ensnaring captives
tangled in darkened folds
tripping through shadow
dissolving in to the broken parts of one
another
shrieks uselessly released in the vacuum
twisting limbs through veins
falling through each other
cloaked in voids of black ink
vicious whispers pouring alongside
creatures
wrapped in empty existence
broken moments of infinity
beating through chambers
pulsing cores of creation
in to unceasing pleasures
scattered selves bury through each other
travelling the ley lines of the universe

PROWL

I wander through dark, twisted hallways
dripping with a hunger never sated
prior feasts all but forgotten
as the desire to hunt tears me from within

inked emptiness pulsates against every torn synapse
while eclipses greedily drink shadow
and viper's kisses scent ether

laughter bleeds through snarled lips
and breath comes ragged and quick
sinews taut, hovering on the edge
of the sweetest destruction

SENSATION

there is
something
bubbling away
under the surface
of me

and I
am trying
to bring it
in to the light
but

it stubbornly
dances
through this viscous
(vicious?)
material of
brimming
subconscious
muck

I know
it has to do
with Feelings
and not
just those ephemeral
nebulous
aortic ones
(though
those are there
too)

but
something
to do
with
sensations
of You

SCULPTURE

---

cold nights
pour through skin
turning souls to ice
carve me open, I beg of you

PRAYER

---

arching backs and spread legs
atop this mountain of ossification
hands reaching towards the unknown
while bowed heads kiss emptied craniums

flames caress along cunts slick with desire
and throats lift to the sky
while incessant incantations and praise
slide down tortured tongues

pleasure sparks through blessed veins
connective circuity crescendos
culminating in an unceasing shriek
while sacrifices writhe in exquisite agony

every last sinew echoing aching release
ricocheting through emptied existence
while lips peel back and teeth flash
and riotous glee fills multiple dimensions

praise hecate
she who ferries us across lands unknown
hail satan
he who blesses us with untold power
and ceaseless pleasure
accept our sacrifices unto you
in exchange for this web of ecstasy

WEBBING

I am in one of
Those Moods
where the world feels
Big
and I am
Amazed and Grateful
for the beautiful people
who have allowed me in to their lives

IV

i am possessed by those most curious and rare

CRAVINGS

I need
to Feel You
I need
your sparking fingertips
trailing electricity
over my skin
I need
your moth soft lips
pressed against me
I need
to feel vibrations
from your voice
echo through my skull
I need
the warmth of your skin
connected to mine
I need
to trace your brows
and cheekbones
and jawline
under my searching fingers
I need
to feel Your Heart
beat
inside me

A GIFT

---

fingertips skim over one another
with small sparking flames
tracing smouldering embers
across smoking skin
stinging limbs with echoes of energy

electricity burns through
soft spinal curves
and curls its way towards hips
and lips
ending in a blazing kiss

sensual shadows greedily gather
and hold us close
as night slips in to our veins

thuds through limbs

and wraps itself along every
last
synapse

until it can no longer be contained

burning hands grasp at electrified skin
as mouths find one another in the dark
to suck shadow from lungs
while connection births the liminal

tongues slide along spines
while minds and hips collide
wholly entwined and lost to creation

pulsing through the dark and empty spaces
where others dare not tread
weaving a web of pleasure and Lust
to ensnare and enrapture

we pour through one another
vessel and host
altar and sacrifice

and eventually emerge anew

forged in the fires of hell
and cooled by the waters of the night

PERCHANCE

I had a dream
where you asked me to dance with you
while I whispered debauchery in your ear

until you decided it was time
to find another use of my tongue
as you gripped my hair
shoved me to my knees
and buried yourself between my lips

WORSHIP

---

wide eyes and bitten lips
beg for release
from untold pleasures
with softened whimpers

eventually granted
writhing in your mouth
at your sole discretion

followed by fingers tangled through tresses
directing your desires
bringing light to murderous eyes
and darkened snarls
displaying carefully contained feral longing

calling forth titans and infernals
audiences to depraved delectation
indulging in praises
uttered from eager lips
summoning their exquisitely painful
pleasures

lost to their void

directed
to take you in hand
and swallow you in your entirety
scything through you
and feasting all that they desired

satisfied by their hollowed hallowed vessels
finally
they watch us rest
eagerly awaiting the next opportunity
for worship

DARKLINGS

---

you are a creature of captivation
using beautiful images
cascading from your fingertips
tumbling off of your tongue
and capturing my mind
not once, or twice,
but infinitely

you are a mirror of scrying
reflecting pools of ink and shadow
that resonate with my own
while we swim in one another's abyss
to depths unbound
voracious with vicious appetites

you are a devil of beauty
moving through the night
finding me walking along ramparts
where I was lost in moonlight
and showing me what it is
to feel safe enough to leave them behind

and I
I stand upon this precipice
extending an offering of myself
an offering of my magic and my power
an offering
of utter connection

DESIRE

how frequently
do you touch yourself to me?

do you do it
while looking at my pictures
in the hours before dawn?

are you enjoying me tonight?

are you curious
about how frequently
I think of you when I touch myself?

should I tell you
that at this moment
I am soaked
with desire
for you?

REVERENCE

---

ave satanas
praise be unto you, my dark lord
your flameshone eyes devour me
and my heart knows no fear

I offer myself as your sacrifice
freely and entirely
my power, yours to wield
my soul, yours to own
my body, yours to claim

tear through my darkness
with your fire and fury
burn me from within
make me your perfect empty vessel
and fill me to overflowing
with your infernal seed

pour the potential of the universe
deep in to the core of me
so that it may corrupt in to shadow
and be borne again in lust and infinity

SACRAMENT

---

wrapped in inked shadows,
desire for devils overwhelms me

palpable night presses against me
responding to my fervent worship
I feel their breath along my neck
smell the musky warm of lust
taste electricity

howling beasts quiet
to play witness to the sacred rite

of my being undone

an ember plucked from between my legs
traces up my spine
sends slivers of flame over my ribs
lighting up my collarbone
outlining my face
before drawing heat back down
down
down

until prayers are but whimpering pleas

a quiet atonement
to be released in to sin

GENESIS

do you feel it?
the way my soul aches for you?
how the universe shatters
when it cries out for you
how the gods quake
at the power that awaits?

does an electric charge build
in the base of your spine
hot with longing
and desire
as flames lick their way along your skin?

do your fingertips light up
burning electric
with insatiable need
to trace jaws
and slide down eager necks?

taste my lungs in your mouth
my skin under your tongue
the nectar of me

wrap yourself around me
slide through me
create and destroy countless universes within me

bind our souls to infinity

MIDNIGHT LONGING

it's 130 am
I miss our midnight chats
where we would send filthy
depraved
erotic
kinky
lustful texts back and forth
for hours
teasing and pleasing ourselves

where you would tell me
to capture
when the moment takes me
so you could relive the night
and drink me in
with your greedy eyes
while your hand moves of its own accord

MIDNIGHT SLUTTERY

it's 2am
and I've been losing myself
to memories of you
fingertips sliding over
across
and through myself
while I pretend they're really yours

perhaps they are
perhaps your soul feels my desire
finds me in the ether
and takes over
gliding itself along my soaking lust
delighting in my shaking skin
entangling itself
with the cries pouring from my throat

V

———————

i become utterly entangled with them,
and i like the way they burrow in to my heart

REVERBERATIONS

softly prising apart
the bars of this cage
I gently probe
and unfold myself
searching
for something I buried so deeply
that even I am no longer sure where it lives

fingertips seeking out
faint
reverberations
softly resonating amongst debris

until
finally
I discover what was lost

softly take it in hand

bring it to the surface

and wordlessly offer it to You

SAFE

I was always
terrified
of gentleness

of showing
soft underbelly
that could be torn to pieces

such vulnerability
opens chasms
to endless depths

but I look at you
and am not afraid
to hold your hand
and step in to the abyss

FROM WITHIN

---

feelings are such curious things
ephemeral, nebulous, powerful beings
so often hidden in plain sight
even while cloaking us whole
we are still oblivious

until suddenly
oh
oh
we see their greatness
and succumb
prey to their whims
on our knees
bathing in their sublime creations

DANCE WITH ME

I dreamt we were dancing
waltzing down a hallway
to music only we could hear
keeping perfect time
as we grinned at one another
the world around us
captivated by choreography
shadows smiling approval
as we laughingly spun around
lost in each other

TIED

---

words always were at my command
but you wrap my tongue in knots

YOU

---

nearly a year
and you still make my heart pound
my tongue twist
and my belly fill with butterflies
nearly a year
and I want you more than ever
nearly a year
and I still feel overwhelming joy
and excitement
every single time I get to see you

CONNECTION

I wasn't looking for you
but out you sprung
and landed in my life

unexpected

but a most welcome surprise

UNADORNED

I didn't expect this
I had no idea that a hello
would turn in to such a beautiful bond

that a simple curiosity
would uncover such a meeting of minds
and that those arresting and kind eyes
would pierce straight through my soul

that a quiet patience
would uncover parts of me
lost to myself
that those gentle hands
would make it so
defences were no longer required

I wasn't expecting this
that I would be wholly embraced
and every last part of me wanted
and seen

and there is so much I want to show you still
I want to make more memories with you
I never want to stop making memories with you
I want us to belly laugh to ridiculous jokes
and I want us to hold each other's softsmol shadows
and I want us to explore the unknown together
and I want us to dance together
and I want us to talk about all things
I want us to never stop talking

I want us

VULNERABLE

---

how do I tell you
that a few lines
spilled across my screen
leaves me with longing
snaking through my core

how do I tell you
that your light
unlocked the shadowed parts of me?

how do I say to you
that I want to bury myself in you
that I need you to hold me
that I think I'm falling in love?

TANGLED

words burrow under my ribcage
trapped within me
they strangle around my throat
and steal my tongue
burning through my nerves
longing to break free
writhing through my core
salting my lips
they make their desperate escape
in to the night air

iloveyouiloveyouiloveyou

VI

---

we exchange a little piece of ourselves,
and further that connection through all the souls we meet

OFFERINGS

come here, darling
lay alongside me
while storms rage

let me kiss you
softly, softly
melt under my fluttering fingertips
let me cloak your soul in soothing shadow

let me trace the bones under your skin
lick the sweat from your brow
and whisper in your ear

come closer
surrender to my abyss
drink of me
taste my inked whispers
as they flow through your veins
and join me in my darkness

drugged and lost
empty and broken
I promise, you won't feel a thing
until you're buried in flame

PERMISSION

---

let these fingertips
trace your mind

let them slide in the core of you

let these lips
find your breath

let them travel over you

let this tongue
steal your soul

let it wrap
around
and through

you

RITUAL

---

traversing the universe
titans ferry ley lines
shrouded in darkness
diving through dimensional voids
creating connections
sparking with electricity

ineffable infernal lords
answer calls of worship
licking embers to coaled caresses
leaving malevolent grins
on the dripping lips
of the possessed

reverent whispers give way
to screams lost to the abyss
magic torn
from willing sacrifice
an offering to devils
to breed with titans
and for the mother of witches
to birth shadows
to their coven of corruption

BAPTISM

---

swollen with pleasure
soaked with desire
crying for release
at the mercy of the merciless

embered fingertips command shadows
conjuring abyssed vortices
gathering darkness ahead of the storm
that lingers in tripwire calms

waiting
to break

unleashing fiery floods
tearing through flesh
screams buried in skin
scrambling to grab anchor
and hold fast
while forces greater than nature
take what they are owed

3 AM

____

thinking about how much I enjoyed
kneeling
in front of you
arching my head back to say hi
(once I realised I was on my knees)
and the amused
yet commanding
hi
you gave me in return

VOWS

---

yielding to power beyond nature
our selves meld and melt
under the watchful gaze of the moon
realigned, we create new constellations
soul to soul, skin to skin, breath to breath

FOUND

---

claw in to this aching vessel
reach through this holy portal
and weave spines through fingertips

let your embers tear through my veins
while these licking flames feast,
devouring screaming caresses

spark over every
aching
atom
while night gathers
and currents thud
through writhing hips

slide through cosmic creation
lost in the inbetween

take your shadows
and pulse
in to
the core of me
forever inking your name
onto immortality

COPULO

---

rapturous union in nomine
malus ecclesia
marking your
dark and reverently lurid impulses non gracia
Desecrating eager vessels in lascivio

DEVIL'S NOTE

---

tendrils of you
snake
along my spine
wrap
my soul in flames
flicker
through my fingertips

every
single
sinew
strains and hums against itself
holding note
while blasphemous prayers
slide through my tongue

hovering
over myself
in delicious torture
carefully
agonisingly
tiptoeing
along the edge

until

i hungrily feast the abyss
wrapping myself through shadow
fervent reverence pouring through my lips

and desire screams frenzied crescendos
through glorious, all consuming infernos

DARKNESS

---

tonight
I long to be hunted
to scramble across leaves
while whipping branches stain my skin

to feel my heart in my throat
choking me in blood
dirt smeared limbs quivering
lungs crying for air I dare not breathe

I crave capture
to fight
viciously
for my life

slowly
losing
control

until I am helpless
and at the mercy of my tormentor

beg
plead
cry
break

and then scream to the gods
knowing they're not listening

COSMIC ENTANGLEMENT

---

feel me
reach out across the night
let my pleasure
snake across your hips
and wrap itself around you

feel this
fire fuelled ache
pulsate through your core

feel my breath
quicken
in your lungs
my heart
pound
in your chest
my blood
course
through your veins

feel these screams wrap around your tongue
these cries burst forth from your lips

feel my body shake and tremble
feel me writhe through you
feel the universe
as it slides between our limbs
and entangles our souls
forever lost to flame
and shadow

VII

---

*filling them with souldreams for reverent desecration
and tender viciousness x*